DISCOVERIES

WAY BEYOND

YOUR VERY

BONES

ALSO BY ROMAN CASTILLEJA

Rowing Home, Lessons From The River Of Life (2021)

DISCOVERIES
WAY BEYOND
YOUR
VERY
BONES

POEMS

ROMAN CASTILLEJA

MYSTIC WATERS
Press

Copyright © 2023 Roman Castilleja.

All rights reserved. This book or any portion thereof may not be reproduced or used in any manner whatsoever without the express written permission of the publisher except for the use of brief quotations in a book review.

Ebook ISBN: 978-1-7338259-3-1
Paperback ISBN: 978-1-7338259-4-8

First printing 2023

Mystic Waters Press
Austin, TX

mysticwaterspress.com

SECTIONS

Love 1

Dream 11

Unknown 31

Heart 49

Revolution 59

Arise 69

Eternal 79

Heaven 89

LOVE

LOVE BLEW US STRAIGHT INTO
AN INTOXICATING DREAM

ONE IN WHICH DEATH WAS NOTHING
BUT A PESKY LITTLE FLEA

TRANSFORMATION

To hold on to the moment is such a burden
To hold on to yesterday can take years, lifetimes
To get past
The rolling tide of waves is too strong
The current is just too strong
It's madness at its core.
The boldness lies in letting go
In moving forward
With the current
The seasons come and go
They bring brilliant new life
To an eternal underlying moment
Life moves
It expands
And so,
        Should we

LOVE

WE ALL ROLL MAGIC

Magic, I tell you,
We all roll magic

The dice seem random
Like a life governed by chance

But within this mysterious riddle
Lies this mesmerizing
Calculated dance

For there is divine order within this game
This eternal connection
Waiting to reveal itself

Waiting
Just waiting
To be availed

All it asks
Is for you to
Live daringly

Throw the dice!

They call

And live this beautiful expression
Where we finally break through

DISCOVERIES WAY BEYOND YOUR VERY BONES

For it is all
And all is you

Magic!

We are indeed magic

    Roll they must

LOVE

THE SEA

Out on the waters of life
Through swift moving currents
Slow bends

Thundering red skies

Lies an energy

We usually hold outside of ourselves
Yet desperately want to be a part of

Where the me
Becomes the we

And the world
The universe
Life...

Waits for some bold moment
One bold moment of change

Where we finally merge back to love

Where the wind kisses your ear
The earth touches your skin
And the energy reawakens your heart

To a bold new reality

Where the mist finally clears
And we move swiftly as One

Through smoky mountains
Orange canyons
Dripping forests
Bony deserts
Fruitful valleys

Back home

To the Sea

LOVE

PARADISE

Out on the edge of this dancing prism
Along this pristine white beach

I once saw
A magnificent beauty

Magnifying through cobalt waters

The moon orchestrating this shadow melody

As she walked

Waves angel dancing
Winds bewitched singing

That feel

Brightly coloring life in

Paradise

And forgive me
For I lost myself

Quietly thinking
Of
You

DREAM

AND HERE WE ARE,
ON THE VERY EDGE OF THE WIND

WHERE YOUR DREAMS
BECOME YOUR REALITY

THE ARRIVAL

This autumn whisper
Inviting us down a new path...

One of change and revitalization
Where the daring hunt wild worlds

Out on that ledge

Where your breath stops
And your heartbeat deepens

Where the stillness lies
And the echoes of yesterday's sorrows
May still linger

Be bold
And take the leap

For tomorrow is gone
And much more lies ahead

Keep moving forward

To that one moment you realize
Where you feel in your very bones
That you're living the very moment

You were born to meet

DREAM

INTO THE SILENCE

Into those moments of nothingness, we share
As we both slip and vanish into the silence

Together into that mysterious abyss

That place

Where a bold new warm breaks open
And every possibility exits

Right next to you

ESCAPE

As the moon made her escape in the cycle of her life
She appeared to light in brilliant wisdom
After her return through the darkness

Such are the rhythm and patterns of life

Our experience
Our mystery

Our destiny

DREAM

THE FLAME

As our eyes gently met

I caught a glimpse
Of an ancient fire

That burning

From the depths of our souls
This bold and brilliant flame

Too big

To hold in a frame

THE RAPTURE

Love

Once whispered into my ear
A fragrance of a melancholy breath

A heartbeat that awoke the soul
A remembrance of a long ago call

Its energy grew deeper within me

A rapture
A dance

That blew my heart wide open
And allowed me to discover you

Oh

This coy dance

Bliss

DREAM

And the heart broke open to a mystical dawn
Dripping the sun, the moon, and the stars

THE PAINTING OF LIFE

Sometimes you want to grab life by its edges
This narrow frame we see
And straighten it as we'd prefer to see it

But this creation we our working on
Will shine its true luster
When one day we can look at it from afar

Where you will see the genius of each stroke
And finally see the magnificence of your art

Keep on painting

For mastery unfolds in its own unique way

DREAM

THE BOLDNESS OF LOVE

As the drops of wine
Made their way down

The fire danced with the blustery wind

Out beyond the edge of the rain
I saw where you and I were willing to go

We drew a deep breath from the great beyond
As adventure lay ahead
And life seemed palpable once again

As our hearts melted into a rhythm
To an ancient echo

And we waltzed into the abyss

LET ME BREATHE YOU

This innate beauty
Has always drawn me to you

I say kill it at its head
Like some huge reptilian python
Just waiting to suffocate my neck

My world says otherwise

For we bloom into dancing flowers
Intoxicating scents

These inhales of some long-lost fragrance

Where you and I just met

Let me breathe you

DREAM

A NEVER-ENDING DAWN

And for a moment
I stepped into the deep abyss
Letting it swallow me whole

I became aware of my blindness
This darkness

Blind to what was indeed real
The veil lifted
And it was ALL bliss

A step into a bold new world

The one within

And love arose
Like a never-ending dawn

DISCOVERIES WAY BEYOND YOUR VERY BONES

A flame dancing wildly
Always burning upwards

So, can we

Breathe

DREAM

WILD HORSES

I once lost my voice to
That never ending movement
Of days gone by

Yet the rhythm
It still beats

Like wild horses
Running

Out into open flames

Rolling prairies
Majestic mountains

I keep running

Still moving forward
Still riding

And my horse and I
Our hearts beat in unison

Always higher ground

We ride forward
Always moving forward

For you must let her run free

GASPING...

I caught a breath
From thin air

Awakening white lilies
Opening

Petal by lovely petal...

With its blissful fragrance
It's moodful dance

Reviving me back from the dead

It was then
That I finally saw her buoyant eyes

DREAM

BORN TO DIE

As the silver moonlit blood
Dripped

Slowly
Slowly

Into my open heart
Love indeed was in the air

Everything is indeed born to die

OUR BEAUTIFUL PATH

Red death danced on the horizon
The siren winds began to howl
The thunder rumbled above us

Darkness was crawling nearer

Yet our lonely road lay straight ahead

Fear lay out in front of us
A cryptic forest

    This was our path

    Calling
    Calling

    Daring our unique name
    This sudden chasm

As we boldly kept moving forward
The mystical heavens arose to greet us

Reflecting the light
We held within

    Oh
    The Divine

Calling for more
More

More!

UNKNOWN

I LOOKED DEEPLY INTO THE UNKNOWN

AND I SAID

YES

DISCOVERIES WAY BEYOND YOUR VERY BONES

THE FLOWER

Daring to play our own tune

Rare is the Being
That breaks free
And freely dances

We yearn to be like that

To be bold
To be daring
To be naturally ourselves

Like a flower
A uniqueness all its own

Dancing fragrance
Dripping petals

Unfolding

Daring
To give it all away

UNKNOWN

IT AWAITS

I've seen the fire
Suspended on your very breath

I've seen the world
That lies deep within your soul

BORDERS AND BOUNDARIES

My grandmother once taught me
Of worlds seen and not seen

    Beyond the known

Where breaths expand and die

    Mystical places

An elegance only she could have taught me
Of borders and boundaries

A world where anything is possible

And love

Just bloomed

UNKNOWN

THE MIRROR

At one point we stood amongst
The paths we carved
The breaths we have taken

A reflection of ourselves

A path carved by pain
The sorrow amongst the trees

Yet at times
We can see past the fog
To a clearing
We have rediscovered

The light we really are

For there is always love
When we think

There is no more

Left to give

DISCOVERIES WAY BEYOND YOUR VERY BONES

THE BEAUTY OF YOUR GIFT

Your smile

The one thing
This universe
Wishes to taste

Give it to them!

Dance your tango
Sing your ballad
Write your poem

And never
        ever look back

UNKNOWN

Your smile removed me from many of my wars

THIS FIELD OF KNOWING

The path of awareness
Moves in that direction

Like a stairway to a brighter room
An expansion of the mind

Hope can be chance,
Faith can include doubt
But knowing
Becomes your reality

Knowing is reality

Out beyond the chatter of the mind
Lies this silent field
Where every possibility exists

A clearing above the clouds
An ancient light

It is in the awareness of knowing
Where the biggest shift takes place

And the path…
Your path

Awaits

UNKNOWN

HOW BEAUTIFUL WERE HER RICHES

Her magic ran deep
Glowing coals of the heart
As she danced
Her own wild sensual dance

DISCOVERIES WAY BEYOND YOUR VERY BONES

Looking deep into the eyes of eternity

I saw that she was made of stars

UNKNOWN

THE NIGHT

As the darkness settled in
To this haunting music

Life seemed to bring on a new depth

The walls closing in on some faraway despair

Alone in the darkness
This fleeting madness

For the moonlight glowed in silence

As the dawn came and spoke loudly

To an awakening

Only few dare

DISCOVERIES WAY BEYOND YOUR VERY BONES

HER ESSENCE

Those eyes she has
They hold light
They hold love
Most of all
They hold me

Right through your bones

UNKNOWN

STATEMENT OF LOVE

And what do they say of Love?
Of that fragrance still lingering in the air?

The one lost long ago
The one that haunts us to this day

What do they say of that?

>They say...
>As the moons move in cycles from some long-ago fire

>They say...
>It can illuminate the darkness long past its burning desire

A beautiful moonlight
Of a long-ago echo

Lighting the way into this beautiful good night

LOVE'S BOUNTY

Come drink from its bountiful beauty
Its dripping nectar

This wild endeavor

Where oceans run deep
And mountains aim high

Love in all its bounty

Melt into its light

And even the sun will envy you

HEART

THE HEART HOLDS A BREATH OF BEAUTY

DARE TO LET IT RUN OPENLY FREE

THE BUTTERFLY

In the glowing silence she stood
Facing toward the winds of life

Looking straight ahead

As the turbulence surrounded
And the chasm seemed unending

Out on the edge of the leaf
A butterfly spread her wings

And leaped into the dark abyss

As the moon watched in envy
She breathlessly flew

And colored the world
With her wings

HEART

A RENEGADE SOUL

A stand amongst the darkness
To become the light, we really are

A beautiful fire...
Emanating, Glowing, Burning

A beacon of love

A light dancing like a flicker of hope...faith
A star amongst the deep dark night

And maybe someday we can navigate our way
Via
A renegade soul burning itself anew

NOTHING LEFT

It's a soft kiss of the wind, the salty feel of the ocean
the bright light of a star

It's the beauty of the dew in the morning light
It's the bright sun's warmth shining down on your skin

It's the breath we take of the air that we cannot see

It's all around you

We arrive when there is nothing left to seek

HEART

WHERE WE BOTH JUST BREATHED

It was always her breath upon the waters
That restarted my indigenous heart

Where we both just dreamed

Where we both just breathed

DISCOVERIES WAY BEYOND YOUR VERY BONES

There's always this rhythm we carry in our soul

Of long-ago rivers
Faraway white sandy beaches

Waves hypnotically calling us home

HEART

A NEW NUMINOUS WORLD

Float away with me to the edge of creation

Where the sky drips of love, madness, and ecstasy

REVOLUTION

HER BREATH BECAME MY BREATH

HER DREAM BECAME MY DREAM

A BEAUTIFUL NEW REVOLUTION

DISCOVERIES WAY BEYOND YOUR VERY BONES

SHE AWOKE

As the dry winds swept across the dark desert
Under the mad skies

She awoke from a deep dream

This boldness we all seek

Where her heart bled a dripped reflection
Onto the parched white sand

Where this river of love
Mirrored the stars, moons, and planets

    Hanging from the deep blue heavens

REVOLUTION

HER ESSENCE

This blooming flower that she was

One of stillness
And colorful depth

A queen totally comfortable in her own kingdom

Totally touching the divine

THE WIND

I once lost something
To an angry wind that took a bite of me

I once thought that death was my only salvation

To heal
To be whole again

I once awoke breathlessly from a dream

To a beautiful river
That flowed into a clear sea

An overwhelming peace
In that deeply alive silence

Way out beyond any thought

Where the wind blew me softly
Back home to the sea

REVOLUTION

TO FEEL ALIVE

That cusp of creativity
That moment of oneness

Where that flame flickers even brighter
Where that radiance burns like the sun

An internal blue flame

A light waiting to expand
Waiting to blind the world

And light it aflame

TIME

And it seemed to me a long time coming

For our beautiful, synchronized heartbeat
Included you

As I breathed
One more time

The mountains moved
The wind danced

All was perfect in this bright world
As we both finally flew free

It was our time

Yours and mine

ARISE

ARISE

FOR DAWN IS NOW UPON US
AND OUR NEW KINGDOM

OF GOLDEN CASTLES
BURSTING GARDENS

ANXIOUSLY

AWAITS

BEAUTY

What is real beauty?

It's that tear drop
The one that fell from your cheek

The one that left a slow trail down your skin

That breathless gasp

That stopped you cold in your tracks
And inspired you to come out of your shell

For beauty is who we are

What we see
What we experience

If only you could just see...

ARISE

NEW BEGINNINGS

Every now and then we come across new frontiers
A fog lying ahead
A place we have yet to experience
To some it may bring a great vulnerability
But in that place of unknowing
Lies a place we have always wanted to go
Chasing a dream
To taste the light

You have always been

DISCOVERIES WAY BEYOND YOUR VERY BONES

AND WHERE WAS YOUR BEAUTY

The one you kept locked in your heart

The one that wanted to run like the wind

The heartbeat that you kept hidden

The thing that just wanted to bloom

ARISE

CHURNING WATERS

Pushing past the chaos
Churning waters

We reached some level of peace

Its beautiful isn't it?

A moment of quietness
Where that bear lies no more

That moment of respite
Where it all ran into place

Early morning
Sunrise

And I smiled
At the beauty I beheld

Majestic creatures roaming

A vast ocean of possibility
Past these wild forests

A place I once knew
A place held on the edge of a breath

DISCOVERIES WAY BEYOND YOUR VERY BONES

BEYOND WORDS

A movement in silence
A way to live beyond words

A moving meditation
A total ballet

That crisp white shirt
Pearls around her neck

Regalness

Of roses I would say
An essence

There is elegance in silence
Beauty in movement

Grace in being

Who we authentically
Are

ETERNAL

TO RUN WITH THE WIND
TO FINALLY TOUCH THEY SKY
TO TASTE THE ETERNAL

DISCOVERIES WAY BEYOND YOUR VERY BONES

LET THAT DAY BE TODAY

One day you're going to look back on your personal movie
To see what played on your screen

The adventure of life makes for great drama
A great story
But who we really are is beyond that

Beyond the sea of emotions
Beyond the body
Beyond the mind

Lies a great mystery
An immovable seer watching it all pass by
And that's the beauty of you and I

Something to Awaken to

One day
One day

ETERNAL

AS THE BRAVE WINDS GENTLY BLEW MY WILD HAIR

I could see the slow river
Making its way across the bend

Reflecting the shimmering trees
Upon the surface of its dark waters

Its gallant song echoing across the canyon
This beautiful silence I now behold

Its depth that I could feel
Deep within my soul

As I felt life in all its wondrous rhythms

This beauty we all hold

DISCOVERIES WAY BEYOND YOUR VERY BONES

GUTS

Mountains will roar
Oceans will sink
Suns will be created

Universes expand

To some flame
Some bold soul

That had the guts to just

Be

ETERNAL

TAKE THE LEAP

Where your breath stops
Where the stillness lies
And the echoes of yesterday's sorrows may still linger

DISCOVERIES WAY BEYOND YOUR VERY BONES

WITHIN

I have learned over time
Over blood shed tears

To let the moon lend me its ear
To let the sun's rays, touch my skin
To let my breath, sink desperately in

To that deepest point in me

And to feel that Aliveness

Within

HEAVEN

THIS HEAVENLY MOMENT
OF AWE
WHERE OUR HEARTS
MERGE
INTO THE POWDERED DEPTHS
OF SILENCE

THERE WE WILL FIND
ETERNAL BEAUTY
THE

NOW

DISCOVERIES WAY BEYOND YOUR VERY BONES

AN INTIMATE MYSTERY

She came with an implacable fire

    Leaving the sky in awe
        The mountains voiceless
            And the rivers dry

HEAVEN

LIVE IT WELL

Out there amongst this field of vibrating energy
Lies you and I
Blinking in and out of existence
Past lives flashing in and out of this plane

A grand flicker

Seize it

Seize every moment you can
Stretch time as far as you can

For life is fleeting
For life is today
For you are life

A beautiful moment of expression
Breaking out into a myriad number of colors

Something felt, tasted, heard, seen,
And lived

Live it well

DISCOVERIES WAY BEYOND YOUR VERY BONES

THE OLD OAK TREE

Out beyond the rolling meadow
Up above the hill
Stands this great Oak tree

It does not worry about the rings
It has created

Its bold branches still stretch
Grand across the sky

Where birds still flock to gather

The beauty of its so-called age
Lies not in its survival
But in its wisdom

As the rings continue to grow
The birds still gather
Its bounty continues to grow taller

As its shadow
Casts a refreshing
Young breeze

HEAVEN

THE ANSWER

We search far and near

Until that moment of total surrender

The place where few go

The space of silence
Where we accept it all
Melt into it all

Out of that moment
The phoenix will rise
Out of the ashes

A total acceptance
A total peace
A total yes

A BEAUTIFUL PERSPECTIVE

And through our perspective
We took it all in

Creating our art
Creating a new vision

Through this daring power
We hold within

The artist

Daring, just daring

To paint it all in

HEAVEN

TO LIVE DANGEROUSLY

Out on the edge of the branch
Lies a rose bud
Daringly growing

The most delicate dance
Of a blooming to behold

Out on the edge of a breath
Lies a bold soul
Wanting to grow

A most harrowing dance
Of a beauty to unfold

A soul on fire

A heart broken
Totally open

Daring to feel it all

DISCOVERIES WAY BEYOND YOUR VERY BONES

Love

This revolution will indeed end
   and begin there

www.ingramcontent.com/pod-product-compliance
Lightning Source LLC
Chambersburg PA
CBHW061730070526
44583CB00024B/3076